New Poems

BOOKS BY KENNETH REXROTH

POEMS

> The Collected Shorter Poems
> The Collected Longer Poems
> Sky Sea Birds Trees Earth House Beasts Flowers
> New Poems
> The Phoenix and the Tortoise

PLAYS

> Beyond the Mountains

CRITICISM & ESSAYS

> The Alternative Society
> American Poetry in the Twentieth Century
> Assays
> Bird in the Bush
> The Classics Revisited
> Communalism, from the Neolithic to 1900
> The Elastic Retort
> With Eye and Ear

TRANSLATIONS

> 100 Poems from the Chinese
> Love and the Turning Year: 100 More Chinese Poems
> The Orchid Boat: The Women Poets of China
>   (*with Ling Chung*)
> 100 French Poems
> Poems from the Greek Anthology
> 100 Poems from the Japanese
> 100 More Japanese Poems (*forthcoming*)
> 30 Spanish Poems of Love and Exile
> Selected Poems of Pierre Reverdy

AUTOBIOGRAPHY

> An Autobiographical Novel

EDITOR

> An Anthology of Pre-literate Poetry
> The Continuum Poetry Series

Kenneth Rexroth
New Poems

A New Directions Book

ACKNOWLEDGMENTS
The sequence *Sky, Sea, Birds, Trees, Earth, House, Beasts, Flowers* was
originally published in a limited edition in 1971 by Unicorn Press, to which
grateful acknowledgment is made. The poems "The Family," "Void Only,"
"No Word," "Suchness," and "It Is a German Honeymoon" all first
appeared in *New Directions in Prose and Poetry* 26 (1973). Four of the
"Translations from the Japanese of Marichiko" (nos. V, IX, X, XI) were
included in *New Directions in Prose and Poetry* 29 (1974).

Manufactured in the United States of America
First published clothbound and as New Directions Paperbook 383 in 1974
Published simultaneously in Canada by McClelland & Stewart, Ltd.

Library of Congress Cataloging in Publication Data

Rexroth, Kenneth, 1905–
  New poems.

  (A New Directions Book)
  I. Title.
PS3535.E923N4   811'.5'2   74–8554
ISBN 0–8112–0550–9
ISBN 0–8112–0551–7 (pbk.)

New Directions Books are published for James Laughlin
by New Directions Publishing Corporation,
333 Sixth Avenue, New York 10014

For Carol

Contents

LOVE IS AN ART OF TIME

NEW POEMS

Now *the starlit moonless Spring*

Now the starlit moonless Spring
Night stands over the Fontaine
De Medicis, and the gold
Fish swim in the cold, starlit
Water. Yesterday, in the
New sunshine, lovers sat by
The water, and talked, and fed
The goldfish, and kissed each other.
I am in California
And evening is coming on.
Now it is morning in Paris
By the Fontaine de Medicis.
And the lovers will come today,
And talk and kiss, and feed the fish,
After they have had their coffee.

THE FAMILY

Late night
Coming back to Melbourne
From a party on the Kangaroo Plains,
We stop the car by a black pool.
The air is immobile, crystalline.
I get out, light a match,
And study my star map.
I blow out the match,
And overhead and before and below me,
Doubled in the unmoving water,
The million stars come on
That I have never seen before
And will never see again.
And there are the two
Daughter universes of my universe,
The Magellanic Clouds—
Two phosphorescent amoebas overhead,
And two in the bottomless water.

NO WORD

The trees hang silent
In the heat . . . . .

      Undo your heart
      Tell me your thoughts
      What you were
      And what you are . . . . .

            Like bells no one
            Has ever rung.

SCHATTEN KUESSE,
SCHATTEN LIEBE

after Heine

Shadow kisses, shadow love,
There is nothing else left now—
Faint electric traces
In the nerve cells of two brains.

The rain falls in the deep night—
Black streets, a distant city—
Far away, too far away—
Yes? Too far away from where?

Too far from time which passes?
Too far from flesh breaking change?
Too far from happiness
Which would not wait an instant?

Two heads alone in dark rooms,
Far apart in rainy night,
Shelter sparks of memory,
Lamps once blazing with kisses.

HAPAX

The Same Poem Over and Over

Holy Week. Once more the full moon
Blooms in deep heaven
Like a crystal flower of ice.
The wide winter constellations
Set in fog brimming over
The seaward hills. Out beyond them,
In the endless dark, uncounted
Minute clots of light go by,
Billions of light years away,
Billions of universes,
Full of stars and their planets
With creatures on them swarming
Like all the living cells on the earth.
They have a number, and I hold
Their being and their number
In one suety speck of jelly
Inside my skull. I have seen them
Swimming in the midst of rushing
Infinite space, through a lens of glass
Through a lens of flesh, on a cup of nerves.
The question is not
Does being have meaning,
But does meaning have being.
What is happening?
All day I walk over ridges
And beside cascades and pools
Deep into the Spring hills.
Mushrooms come up in the same spot
In the abandoned clearing.
Trillium and adder's tongue
Are in place by the waterfall.

A heron lifts from a pool
As I come near, as it has done
For forty years, and flies off
Through the same gap in the trees.
The same rush and lift of flapping wings,
The same cry, how many
Generations of herons?
The same red tailed hawks court each other
High on the same rising air
Above a grassy steep. Squirrels leap
In the same oaks. Back at my cabin
In the twilight an owl on the same
Limb moans in his ancient language.
Billions and billions of worlds
Full of beings larger than dinosaurs
And smaller than viruses, each
In its place, the ecology
Of infinity.
I look at the rising Easter moon.
The flowering madrone gleams in the moonlight.
The bees in the cabin wall
Are awake. The night is full
Of flowers and perfume and honey.
I can see the bees in the moonlight
Flying to the hole under the window,
Glowing faintly like the flying universes.
What does it mean. This is not a question, but
      an exclamation.

CONFUSION OF THE SENSES

Moonlight fills the laurels
Like music. The moonlit
Air does not move. Your white
Face moves towards my face.
Voluptuous sorrow
Holds us like a cobweb
Like a song, a perfume, the moonlight.
Your hair falls and holds our faces.
Your lips curl into mine.
Your tongue enters my mouth.
A bat flies through the moonlight.
The moonlight fills your eyes
They have neither iris nor pupil
They are only globes of cold fire
Like the deers' eyes that go by us
Through the empty forest.
Your slender body quivers
And smells of seaweed.
We lie together listening
To each other breathing in the moonlight.
Do you hear? We are breathing. We are alive.

BLUE SUNDAY

Chestnut flowers are falling
In the empty street that smells
Of hospitals and cooking.
The radio is breaking
Somebody's heart somewhere
In a dirty bedroom. Nobody
Is listening. For ten miles
In either direction
The houses are all empty.
Nobody lives in this city.
Outside the city limits
Are green and white cemeteries.
Nobody is in the graves.
At very long intervals
The broken cast iron fountain
In the courtyard sneezes and spurts.
In the dirty bedroom
Three young whores are shooting dice.
At very long intervals
One of them speaks to the dice.
Otherwise they are silent.
After the chestnut blossoms
Have all fallen the yellow
Sun will set and stars shine
Over the empty city
And papers blow down the street.

I DREAM OF LESLIE

You entered my sleep,
Come with your immense,
Luminous eyes,
And light brown hair,
Across fifty years,
To sing for me again that song
Of Campion's we loved so once.
I kissed your quivering throat.
There was no hint in the dream
That you were long, long since
A new arrivéd guest,
With blithe Helen, white Iope and the rest—
Only the peace
Of late afternoon
In a compassionate autumn
In youth.
And I forgot
That I was old and you a shade.

EDUCATION

Now to the dry hillside,
Terraced with crumbling limestone,
Where there were vineyards long ago,
Evening comes cool and violet
Under the olive trees, and only
The almond blossoms and the first stars
Are alight. Your fine lean hand
Like a spindle of light
Moves as you talk, as if
You were conducting a slow music.
What are you talking about?
You are explaining everything to me—
The abandoned olive grove,
The walls older than the Romans,
The flowering almond tree,
And the twilight darkening
Around the stars and around
You speaking lips and moving hand.

PRIVACY

Dense fog shuts down
Between the hills.
I step out of my cabin.
You'd never know
It was in the midst of a forest.
Fog curls in the lighted doorway like smoke.
I hear the raccoon rustling
In the invisible thicket.
The cool dampness creeps under my clothes.
I thought I heard a car
Come up the road below me.
I walk cautiously through the fog
To the edge of the cutting.
I can see nothing.
Suddenly I hear
Beneath my feet
A man and a woman cry out with love.

PARITY

My uncle believed he had
A double in another
Universe right here at hand
Whose life was the opposite
Of his in all things—the man
On the other side of zero.
Sometimes they would change places.
Not in dreams, but for a moment
In waking, when my uncle
Would smile a certain sly smile
And pause or stagger slightly
And go about his business.

IT IS A GERMAN HONEYMOON

They are stalking humming birds
The jewels of the new world
The rufous hummingbird dives
Along his parabola
Of pure ether. We forgot—
An imponderable and
Invisible elastic
Crystal is the womb of space.
They wait with poised cameras
Focused telescopic lens
Beyond the crimson trumpet vine.
He returns squealing against
The sky deeper than six billion
Light years, and plunges through sun
Blaze to the blood red flower womb.
A whirling note in the lens of space.
"Birds are devas," says Morris
Graves, "They live in a world
Without Karma." No grasping,
No consequence, only the
Grace of the vectors that form
The lattices of the unending
Imponderable crystal.
The blond and handsome young man
And woman are happy, they
Love each other, when they have
Gone around the world they will
Sit in the Grunewald and
Look at a picture of a
California hummingbird.
Nobody can swim across
The Great River. Turn your back
And study the spotted wall.
Turn around on the farther shore.
Nine dice roll out, one by one.

The mouse eats them. They never were.
The hundred flowers put their
Heads together, yellow stamens and
Swelling pistils. Between them
In midspace they generate
A single seed. You cannot
Find it in a telescope.
Found, you could not see it in
An electron microscope.

BEI WANNSEE

Evening twirling
In a thousand thanks
The spindle glows
Pale water
Copper flows
Swans
Sails cluster and part again
Ripples
Mouths kiss and suck and part
The sun breaks in bands of haze
A silent exclamation
A white bird
A naked joy
A thousand thanks
The water becomes imaginary
The swans go
The lights come
Paler than water
The perfume of the bed of stock
Billows down the lawn and out
Over the water
Past the motionless scarves of weeping willow
And up from the glittering boat
A flute spirals and says quietly
Like a waving light

A blonde

Come

A thousand thanks
A waving light.

RED MAPLE LEAVES

The maple leaves are brilliant
Over the tree lined streets.
The deep shade is filled
With soft ruddy light.
Soon the leaves will all have fallen.
The pale winter sunlight
Will gleam on snow covered lawns.
Here we were young together
And loved each other
Wise beyond our years.
Two lifetimes have gone by.
Only us two are left from those days.
All the others have gone with the years.
We have never seen each other since.
This is the first time I have ever come back.
I drive slowly past your home,
Around the block again and once again.
Beyond the deep pillared porch
Someone is sitting at the window.
I drive down by the river
And watch a boy fishing from the bridge
In the clear water amongst
Falling and floating leaves.
And then I drive West into the smoky sunset.

IT TURNS OVER

The lightning does not go out
But stays on in the sky all night
A waterfall of solid white fire
Red hands speak
In deaf and dumb language
Their green shadows
Projected on the orange sky
All the worms come out
All the eggs hatch
All the clouds boil away
Only Orion all alone in the zenith
Of midsummer midnight.

STAR AND CRESCENT

The air has the late summer
Evening smell of ripe foliage
And dew cooled dust. The last long
Rays of sunset have gone from
The sky. In the greying light
The last birds twitter in the leaves.
Far away through the trees, someone
Is pounding something. The new
Moon is pale and thin as a
Flake of ice. Venus glows warm
Beside it. In the abode
Of peace, a bell calls for
Evening meditation.
As the twilight deepens
A voice speaks in the silence.

LA VIE EN ROSE

Fog fills the little square
Between Avenue du Maine
And the Gaité Montparnasse.
I walk around and around,
Waiting for my girl.
My footsteps echo
From the walls
Of the second storeys.
Deep in the future
My ghost follows me,
Around and around.

VOID ONLY

Time like glass
Space like glass
I sit quiet
Anywhere Anything
Happens
Quiet loud still turbulent
The serpent coils
On itself
All things are translucent
Then transparent
Then gone
Only emptiness
No limits
Only the infinitely faint
Song
Of the coiling mind
Only.

SUCHNESS

In the theosophy of light,
The logical universal
Ceases to be anything more
Than the dead body of an angel.
What is substance? Our substance
Is whatever we feed our angel.
The perfect incense for worship
Is camphor, whose flames leave no ashes.

Late half moon

Late half moon
High over head.
Shaka merges with Tara.
The dark bride possesses her lover.
Two moaning owls fly from the
Pine to the cypress.
The largest telescope
Reveals more nebulae
Outside our galaxy
Than stars within it—
There are more cells
In a single brain.
The sands of all the seas
Have a number.
The red shift—
The mortal soul
In its immortal body.
Light tires and wears out,
Travelling through space.
The owls mate
In the moonfilled dawn.

YOUR BIRTHDAY IN THE
CALIFORNIA MOUNTAINS

A broken moon on the cold water,
And wild geese crying high overhead,
The smoke of the campfire rises
Toward the geometry of heaven—
Points of light in the infinite blackness.
I watch across the narrow inlet
Your dark figure comes and goes before the fire.
A loon cries out on the night bound lake.
Then all the world is silent with the
Silence of autumn waiting for
The coming of winter. I enter
The ring of firelight, bringing to you
A string of trout for our dinner.
As we eat by the whispering lake,
I say, "Many years from now we will
Remember this night and talk of it."
Many years have gone by since then, and
Many years again. I remember
That night as though it was last night,
But you have been dead for thirty years.

THE FLOWER SUTRA

Deep drowsy shade under the broad leaves,
The dusty plain far below dim with haze,
Picking flowers—bush clover, gold banded lily,
Bell flower, wild pink, while a mountain cuckoo
Flutters about, watching me and crying,
"Kegonkyo."

EARTH SKY SEA
TREES BIRDS
HOUSE
BEASTS FLOWERS

Cold before dawn

Cold before dawn,
Off in the misty night,
Under the gibbous moon,
The peacocks cry to each other,
As if in pain.

A *cottage in the midst*

A cottage in the midst
Of a miniature forest.
The only events are the distant
Cries of peacocks, the barking
Of more distant dogs
And high over head
The flight of cawing crows.

Past and future fall away

Past and future fall away.
There is only the rose and blue
Shimmer of the illimitable
Sea surface.
No place.
No time.

Slowly the moon rises

Slowly the moon rises
Over the quiet sea.
Slowly the face of my beloved
Forms in my mind.

Moonless night

Moonless night.
In the black heavens
The eye goes ten million miles.
Melancholy fills the heart.

Spring puddles give way

Spring puddles give way
To young grass.
In the garden, willow catkins
Change to singing birds.

A dawn in a tree of birds

A dawn in a tree of birds.
Another.
And then another.

Past midnight

Past midnight,
In the dark,
Under the winter stars,
Tendrils of ice
Creep through the duckweed.

As the years pass

As the years pass,
The generations of birds pass too.
But you must watch carefully.
The same towhees and jays
Seem to have been in the same places
To thousands of generations of men.

In the dark forest the whisper

In the dark forest the whisper
Of a million leaves.
On the deep sea the sigh
Of a million waves.

A long lifetime

A long lifetime
Peoples and places
And the crisis of mankind—
What survives is the crystal—
Infinitely small—
Infinitely large—

THE CITY OF THE MOON

for *Kimiko Nakazawa*

I

The sun sets as the moon
Rises. The red maple leaves
Fade to the color
Of an aging heart.

II

In the fine warm rain
Falling over the late turning
Maple leaves, an uguisu
Sings as if in Spring.

III

The East Wind brings clouds
And rain. In the ruffled pond
Happy goldfish play.
But it is the end
Of the eleventh month, warm,
Unseasonably.

IV

Although I am far from home
The red maple leaves
Over the old pond
Of the temple garden
Are falling with the
Plum leaves by my own window.

V

No, I did not say a word.
It is useless to
Pretend that the sound of rain
Is a human voice.

I shall have the banana
Trees by my window destroyed.
The pattering of
The rain sounds like the weeping
Of all the spirits
Of the air, and the
Wind tearing the leaves sounds like
The sound of ripped silk.

VI

In a waking dream,
A princess of the old time
Comes to me over
The twisting foot bridge,
Through the midst of the marsh
Of yellow iris
And lightly touches my lips.
The delicate sensation
Of utter intimacy
Lingers as the light goes out,
And the leaves of the iris
Murmur and rustle
In the twilight wind.

VII

Although the great plane
Flies away toward the sun,
The morning raven
Will still perch on the balcony
Of the Ueno Park of the heart.

VIII

THE NEW YEAR

Midnight passes—
A new year—Orion strides
Into the warm waves
Westward to Yamashina
Where the red and gold
Of a glorious autumn
Lie under the snow.

IX

ICHŌ

The plane rises through
Snowing clouds. Far beneath two
Autumn ginkos blaze,
Burning gold in the harsh
Night lights of Tokyo.

X

Buddha took some Autumn leaves
In his hand and asked
Ananda if these were all
The red leaves there were.
Ananda answered that it
Was Autumn and leaves
Were falling all about them,
More than could ever
Be numbered. So Buddha said,
"I have given you
A handful of truths. Besides
These there are many
Thousands of other truths, more
Than can ever be numbered."

XI

Clouds are the thoughts of
Heaven. It is difficult
To read the thoughts of
Other people, but you can
Always read those of heaven.

Kyoto
November 1972

TRANSLATIONS FROM
THE JAPANESE OF MARICHIKO

I

The full moon of Spring
Rises out of the Void
And pushes aside the
Net of stars—a crystal ball
On pale velvet set with gems.

Marichiko

II

This Spring Mercury
Is farthest from the sun and
Burns, a lonely spark
In the last glow of sunset
Over the uncountable
Sands and waves of the
Illimitable ocean.

Marichiko

III

Early spring this year—
Pittosporum, plums, peaches,
Almonds, mimosa,
All bloom at once. Under the
Full moon, night smells like your body.

Marichiko

IV

It is the time when
The wild geese return. Between
The setting sun and
The rising moon, a line of
Brant write the character "heart."

Marichiko

V

Who is there? Me.
Me who? I am me. You are you.
You take my pronoun
And we are us.

Marichiko

VI

As I came from the
Hot bath, you took me before
The long mirror, my
Breasts quivered in your hands, my
Buttocks shivered against you.

Marichiko

VII

Your tongue thrums and moves
Into me, and I become
Hollow and blaze with
Whirling light, like the inside
Of a vast expanding pearl.

Marichiko

VIII

I scream as you bite
My nipples and orgasm
Drains my body as if I
Had been cut in two.

Marichiko

IX

I wish I could be
Kannon of the thousand heads
To kiss you, and Kannon
Of the thousand arms
To embrace you.

Marichiko

41

X

I cannot forget
The perfumed dusk inside the
Tent of my black hair,
As we awoke in the dawn
To love after a night of love.

Marichiko

XI

Every morning
I wake alone, dreaming
My arm is your sweet flesh
Pressing my lips.

Marichiko

XII

Love me. At this moment
We are the happiest
People in the world.

Marichiko

IMITATIONS OF THE CHINESE

for Ling

THE FALL OF CH'OU

Jade pendants chime before the dawn audience.
Peach blossoms drown in the swollen stream.
Barbarian fires overwhelm the guards.
Together two skylarks rise towards heaven.
Two hearts singing like chiming jade.

ERINNERUNG

At the door of my thatched hut,
Buried deep in the forested mountains,
The wind in the ancient ginko tree
Sounds like the rustle of brocaded silk.

LOST LOVE

Geese fly from North to South
You are far away in
The East. The West wind will carry
A message to the East, but
Here in the Far West, the East
Wind never blows.

MORE TRANSLATIONS
FROM THE CHINESE

THE CHERRY TREE

The cherry as spring comes on
Will bloom again by the same pool.
Man keeps the love of the years that are gone
The flowers return to the same branches.

Anonymous

A RINGING BELL

I lie in my bed,
Listening to the monastery bell.
In the still night
The sound re-echoes amongst the hills.
Frost gathers under the cold moon.
Under the overcast sky,
In the depths of the night,
The first tones are still reverberating
While the last tones are ringing clear and sharp.
I listen and I can still hear them both,
But I cannot tell when they fade away.
I know the bondage and vanity of the world.
But who can tell when we escape
From life and death?

Ch'ang Yu

THANK YOU FOR
YOUR LETTER

The letter you sent me touched my heart.
The paper was decorated with a pair of magpies.
Now I think always of the magpies who fly with joined wings.
I do not mind that your letter was so short.

The Poetess Ch'ao Li-houa

The fireflies dance in the dark

The fireflies dance in the dark
Like sparkling atoms.
The last song of the crickets
In the evening
Awakes all the old memories.
Suddenly the moon vanishes
Behind the roof top.
The wind growls in the stove.
Threads of frost crystals
Appear on the cold bamboo leaves.

Emperor Ch'ien-wen of Liang

GETTING UP IN WINTER

Winter morning.
Pale sunlight strikes the ceiling.
She gets out of bed reluctantly.
Her nightgown has a bamboo sash.
She wipes the dew off her mirror.
At this hour there is no one to see her.
Why is she making up so early?

Emperor Ch'ien-wen of Liang

AUTUMN

A cup of clear wine
Sweet as honey.
A girl with braids
Black as a crow,
Why ask if Spring
Is lovelier than Autumn?
I have never been able
To decide if peach blossoms
Were prettier than chrysanthemums.

Ch'in Kuan

SPRING

Light clouds, high noon,
Beautiful weather.
There is no wind
In the old willow tree.
The blue green jade leaves
Are perfectly still.
I read lazily,
Scratching my head.
Beyond the wall
I can hear
Now and then
The flute of a cakeseller.

Ch'in Kuan

ALONG THE GRAND CANAL

Hoar frost has congealed
On the deck
Of my little boat.
The water
Is clear and still.
Cold stars beyond counting
Swim alongside.
Thick reeds hide the shore.
You'd think you'd left the earth.
Suddenly there breaks in
Laughter and song.

Ch'in Kuan

SPRING BEGINS

Golden murmur of new poplar leaves
On the swaying branches.
The Spring breeze blows through the painted hall.
My head clears from wine.
I lay aside my fan
And sing softly to myself.
New snow blows through the bamboo blinds—
But it smells to me like peach blossoms.

Ch'in Kuan

STROLLING IN THE
MOONLIGHT

Me and my cane, that's two of us.
We walk in the moonlight.
Our shadow makes three.
I don't know where my family
Have all gone to.
Now that I am old
I'll have to take care of myself.

Ch'in Kuan

SORROW

I grew up without the care of parents.
My heart is shut away in its sorrow.
Already my hair is turning grey
And I wander all alone in an empty house.
My life has been so hard and troubled
It is difficult for me to tell it over.
When I was seventeen I lost my husband
At eighteen my only son died.
Now they sleep forever in the cemetery
Under the weeping willows
Under summer dew and winter snow.
Under roofs of grass and weeds.
Why are our lives so unequal?
Why is the will of heaven so capricious?
There is no one but myself to comfort me.
People avoid me because of my sadness.
I watch the birds roosting together on the same branch
And I can never put my empty nest out of my mind.

The Poetess Fang Wei-yi

OVER

In the old days,
You and me,
We were close as a man and his shadow.
Now when you are with me,
You are vague as a cloud.

In the old days,
You and me
We were like a song and its echo, one to the other.
Now when you are with me
We are like dead leaves falling from the branch.

In the old days,
You and me,
We were like gold in quartz, without spot or blemish.
Now when you are with me
We are like dead stars whose splendor is long gone.

Fou Hinan

HOPELESSNESS

When I look in the mirror
My face frightens me.
How horrible I have become!
When Spring comes back
Weakness overcomes me
Like a fatal sickness.
I am too slothful
To smell the new flowers
Or to powder my own face.
Everything exasperates me.
The sadness which tries me today
Adds itself to the accumulated
Sorrows of the days that are gone.
I am frightened by the weird cries
Of the nightjars that I cannot
Shut out from my ears.
I am filled with bitter embarrassment
When I see on the curtains
The shadows of two swallows making love.

Li Ch'ing-chao

DEEP NIGHT

Deep night. I sing, alone in the dark.
The music of the strings reveals my heart.
Frost creeps through the curtains of the bed.
The wind rustles in the trees.
The bright lamp has gone out.
The bright face is gone forever.
I sing your poems
To the tunes you used to sing.
Now the music brings only the deepest sorrow.

Pao Ch'ao

SINCE YOU WENT AWAY

After you were gone
The moon came and shone
In the vacant window.
I thought of you as a flower
Carried off by the wind,
That went its way,
And can never turn back.

The Poetess Shu Ch'i-siang

DRINKING ON THE LAKE,
FAIR WEATHER, THEN RAIN

Light floods the waves
It is a beautiful day.
Suddenly dark clouds
Hide the mountains.
The rain is refreshing, too.
Lake of the West, Lady of the West—
They are incomparable.
Lightly painted, heavily made up
I find most girls equally attractive.

Su Tung P'o

ON A PAINTING BY WANG,
THE CLERK OF YEN LING

The slender bamboo is like a hermit.
The simple flower is like a maiden.
The sparrow tilts on the branch.
A gust of rain sprinkles the flowers.
He spreads his wings to fly
And shakes all the leaves.
The bees gathering honey
Are trapped in the nectar.
What a wonderful talent
That can create an entire Spring
With a brush and a sheet of paper.
If he would try poetry
I know he would be a master of words.

Su Tung P'o

Flower petals drift over the courtyard

Flower petals drift over the courtyard
Moss creeps into the rooms
Everything was said on both sides
Now there is only a musty smell in the air.

                    Wang Ch'ang-ling

COMPLAINT OF A YOUNG GIRL

Nobody but me can know the sorrow that wrings me.
Weeping I return to my obscurity
I keep from the past only bitterness
In the present there is only black emptiness.

I send you back your gifts, jewels, earrings,
The fur jacket I wore in the old days,
You can tie up a broken string
But never put back together a broken heart.

Wang Chung-ju

The cuckoo's call

The cuckoo's call, though
Sweet in itself, is hard to
Bear, for it cries
"Perishing! Perishing!"
Against the Spring.

Wang Hung Kung

THINKING OF HIS DEAD WIFE

The autumn winds begin.
White clouds drift across the sky.
The leaves turn yellow and fall.
Wild geese pass over head towards the South.
Autumn iris are in bud.
Chrysanthemums start to bloom.
I think of the girl I love
Who I can never forget.
I take the ferry boat
Across the turbulent river.
The prow plunges in the current,
Through the foaming waves.
I listen to the flutes and drums.
I listen to the songs of the rowers.
Everybody is so happy.
Only my heart is full of sorrow.
If I cannot bear this when I am strong and young,
What will happen when I grow old?

Emperor Wu of Han

For his joyful homecoming

For his joyful homecoming
I put on my embroidered girdle
Over my brocade dress
Decorated with symbols of faithful love.
Full of passion he came
On the night of the full moon.
Laughing, we played at clouds and rain
Until the sun came up.

Emperor Wu of Liang

Last autumn ended

Last autumn ended
Just a little while ago.
Now it is the beginning
Of the autumn of another year.
Heavy dewfall,
Cold air drains down the mountain.
Gusts of wind
The nostalgia of the crickets' last song.
Flocks of chattering birds
Prepare to leave our forest.
Soon the fishes will hide
Deep under the waterweeds.
Sometimes the sun breaks through the fog.
Other times the low clouds
Growl with thunder.

Emperor Yang of Sui

CHINESE POEMS

Translated by Kenneth Rexroth and Ling Chung

TRAVELLING IN HSIANG COUNTY

Flying flowers from both shores
Glow red on our boat.
In half a day we speed
100 li between elm lined banks.
I lie and watch the sky
Full of unmoving clouds
And do not realize
Both I and the clouds
Are borne together on the East Wind.

Ch'en Yu I

COMPOSED IN A DREAM

On the road of Spring, rain multiplies the flowers,
And the flowers kindle the mountain into Spring.
I follow the brook to its hidden source
Among a thousand golden orioles.

Before my eyes the flying clouds
Change into dragons dancing in the blue sky.
Drunk, lying in the shade
Of the old rattan blinds,
I can't tell North from South.

Ch'in Kuan
[1048–1100]

WRITTEN FOR KO YAH CH'ING

My lord, you live beside the river
In a painted palace
And I live at the corner of the sea.
My tears fall in the sea
And the tide carries them
Before your tower
Where they stop in the flowing water.

Han Chu

WEST VILLAGE

There are temples everywhere
But in West Village
There are only eight or nine families.
I catch some fish,
But there is no place to sell them.
I buy some wine,
And eat and drink
Amongst the flowering rushes.

Kuo Hsiang Cheng

EVENING VIEW FROM
WILLOW BRIDGE

I hear a fish jump in the little pool.
I wait for my crane
To return from the thick woods.

The idle clouds
Will not make rain
But fly off to
The blue peaks.

Lu Yu

EXILE IN JAPAN

On the balcony of the tower
I play my flute and watch
The Spring rain.
I wonder
If I ever
Will go home and see
The tide bore
In Chekiang River again.
Straw sandals, an old
Begging bowl, nobody
Knows me. On how many
Bridges have I trampled
The fallen cherry blossoms?

Su Man Shu

ON THE RIVER

The West wind ruffles the water
And scatters the last red flowers over the river.
A horizontal flute blows a friend's farewell,
Eastward across the jumbled hills.

Wang An Shih

BOATING ON WU SUNG RIVER

The setting sun leaks through the sparse,
Slender, flowering rushes.
For half a day I've been alone
Chanting poems
And haven't crossed the river.
Only the egrets have understood me.
Time after time they come
Stand on one leg and look in the boat window.

Wang Yu Ch'en

INDEX OF TITLES, FIRST LINES, & AUTHORS TRANSLATED

Poem titles are printed in *italic* type, names of authors translated are in LARGE AND SMALL capital letters.

POETRY/ISBN: 0-8112-0551-7

KENNETH REXROTH
New Poems

"In his poetry," writes critic Morgan Gibson of Kenneth Rexroth, "he attains—not by ego or will, but through the grace of imagination—communion with nature and those he loves; and, in a transcendent community of love, he discovers himself as being responsible for all." This sense of what is universal, his prophetic embrace of all being and beings, is the moving spirit in New Poems, Rexroth's first major collection since Love and the Turning Year: One Hundred More Poems from the Chinese (1970). These ninety-one pieces—original poems, adaptations, and translations—include much previously unpublished work, as well as Sky Sea Birds Trees Earth House Beasts Flowers, brought out in a limited edition by Unicorn Press. Rendered from the Chinese, some in collaboration with Ling Chung, are poems from the classic writers and three by Rexroth himself. Translations from the Japanese focus on the short, sensual poems of the contemporary woman poet Marichiko, who takes her pen name from Marichi, the Hindu goddess of the dawn. New Poems is but the latest display of the broad, striking range of Rexroth's poetic powers.

[Some other Kenneth Rexroth Paperbooks: Assays, NDP113, $2.25; An Autobiographical Novel, NDP281, $2.95; Beyond the Mountains, NDP384, $3.25; Bird in the Bush, NDP80, $3.95; Collected Longer Poems, NDP309, $2.75; Collected Shorter Poems, NDP243, $2.95; Love and the Turning Year, NDP308, $1.95; 100 Poems from the Chinese, NDP192, $1.75; 100 Poems from the Japanese, NDP147, $1.75.]

Cover photograph of Kenneth Rexroth by Margo Moore;
design by Gertrude Huston

A NEW DIRECTIONS PAPERBOOK   NDP383 $2.95

'An exuberant study
of the phenomenon.'
The Times

We'll always have "Casablanca"

The Life, Legend, and Afterlife
of Hollywood's Most Beloved Movie

NOAH ISENBERG